Days like this

Madeleine Martin

BookLeaf Publishing

Presentation by *BookLeaf Publishing*

Web: www.bookleafpub.com

E-mail: info@bookleafpub.com

ISBN: 9789395950725

First edition 2022

To my sisters, my children and my beautiful granddaughters.

ACKNOWLEDGEMENT

Thank you to my young friend Jagriti, who introduced me to this means of publishing a handful of my poems; and to the richness of my life, my friends, my family, (those lost and gained,) who have inspired this anthology.

PREFACE

Poetry is a mindful way of expressing your emotions and thoughts without involving anyone else. It exercises your brain and releases your demons without causing any further damage to you, or to the world.

It doesn't pollute or poison. It enables language to have meanings on several planes, whatever the writer's intentions were; when read by others it can only be interpreted by the reader's own context, so it can touch many different people on many different levels and generate a greater depth of meaning.

Woman of the world

Worked hard all my life to fund my social station,
Waitressed through my teenage years in any paid location,
Now I own my house, my car, don't need a free donation,
I'm an independent woman of the world.

Successfully qualified from my western education,
Been both a nurse and teacher, rewarding each vocation,
Two caring jobs, careers that supported half the nation,
I'm a contributing woman of the world.

I travel everywhere by international aviation,
US, Asia, Africa explored each destination,
Culture, history, cuisine I taste with jubilation,
I'm a well-seasoned woman of the world.

Not lost my kids' lives through a corrupt organization,
Nor been naked, cold or hungry; suffered any deprivation,

Never forced to flee oppression from the land of my creation,
I'm a lucky, privileged, blessed, sheltered, loved…
Woman of the world.

Ode to Alcohol 1

Pour me another prosecco
Buy me another beer
A crisp glass of dry white wine
Will always bring me cheer

I think it was UB40 that said,
"Red red wine goes to my head"
But "makes me forget" the fact
That it is hastening my death
At 4.30 in the morning
I wake up full of fear
With cramp, mightmares and the horror that
My end is drawing near
And I've so much more to live for
My family, my friends
But I carry on downing poison
And the guilt just never ends
And when I'm down or lonely
And no one is around
I pour myself another drink-
It's company, I've found
It dulls the senses, makes me feel
Vivacious, pretty, funny
And while it travels my bloodstream
The day is always sunny.

So
Pour me another prosecco
Buy me another beer
Several large glasses of dry white wine
Will always bring me cheer.

Words from my right knee

Why do you have to run and run?
Is it to impress? Get into that dress?
By losing a pound or two?

Why do you ski through powder and slush?
Why the big rush to
Conquer and crush
And compete to extremes?
Pistes are less fuss.

I've bent over forwards for you
Whenever you've asked
I dive and I dangle
Rotate at an angle
I lose my protection when changing direction!
I'm starting to cry when the impact is high.
But I'm feeling the strain
And I'm giving you pain,
So I'm begging you please!
Be kind to your knees!
(They'll probably crack. Then you'll be back, to
limping the floor-
(Like Terry next door.)

*Terry, next door neighbour has bad knees and sits in a chair in front of the tv all day.

Haglund's deformity

I can’t tell you how bad it can feel,
To have a lump on the back of your heel,
First it throbs; then it burns
Seems to take them both in turns,
A tender spot,
hard and hot,
I can’t tell you the enormity
Of living with a Haglund’s deformity.

I like a round of golf and adore playing tennis,
But this lump on my heel is becoming a menace,
Pulls on my tendon, rubs on my shoe,
Makes me more miserable than covid or flu’
(Both of which last only a week or two)
A tender spot,
hard and hot,
I can’t tell you the enormity
Of living with a Haglund’s deformity.

Fishbowl

(When I started to go off my ex-boyfriend as he discussed his ex)

Bunny boiler
Is what he called her-
He only has a fish,
Which spends its time
Swimming round and round
In a Perspex, convex dish.

Over the gravel- then
In and out the weed,
Up to the surface
When it's time to feed
Then another hundred
Laps to achieve.

If it could speak
What would it say?
"It's a tedious means
Of spending my day so I
Do a one eighty and
Lap the other way."

Perhaps one day
She'll revolt and try
To leap out of the water
And sail through the sky
(Only to flop on the carpet and die.)

Did he once call her
His darling, his sweet?
Cook her a favourite meal
for a treat?
'til she clicked that
They never went out of his street?

She probably flicked her tail and fins,
And chanced the final spoiler,
Angled for a change of scene,
Pushed the lid off his tureen,
And became the bunny boiler.

Learning French

Veux-tu, ou
Voulez-vous- it
Comes so easily to you
C'est, il est
Comme-ca, comme-ci
Just don't come easily to me
I'm writing you a billet-doux,
I hope this will appeal to you
Of bon mots shared through our small time
Enshrining them in one short rhyme
So hard to have a pas de deux,
with a French disabled raconteur
no femme fatale, no air of chic
certainement pas fantastique,
But with a little "coup de main"
From one who has "cherchez la femme"
She may become a force majeure,
Reciting cliches by the heure
Like coup de foudre, bon voyage,
Gateau, novel et sabotage.

Entre-nous, Pour un fait accompli-
Marche doucement avec moi, merci.

Alien Invasion

Big fat white nodule
In my mother's lung
Gloating with spite
We thought we'd chased you out
With all the rest from
My mother's breast

But you hid in forgotten cells
Travelled down secret pathways where
The radium didn't penetrate
Bided your time by taking
The scenic route,
Setting up home as a
Bronchiole squatter,
Rotting away the fresh airways,
Blocking the circulation and forcing out
The genuine lodgers,
The humble alveoli
Inviting your mafioso mates to shack up there
too.
And multiply without a licence.

When you are still very young

Don't gripe or moan about your age,
Each day is just another stage,
Enjoy life's moments, embrace, rejoice,
Time is imperative to gain your true voice.

Your journey through each passing year,
Builds experience cementing your presence here,
Knowledge acquired to develop your skills-
Allows you to surf disappointments and thrills,
Without these- life is empty, vacuous, dull-
Feeding your inner soul makes you beautiful.

So, when you lose your youthful glow
Your body heads south, the wrinkles show,
If you've lived each minute as your last,
You will celebrate the richness of your past.

2nd September 2022
For J.C. on her 24th birthday! From JH, (40 years older than you and still loving life, still looking forwards, after my Beatles' birthday)

If Maisie could speak

When she wakes me every morning
I'm sofa- bound; zonked out!
But I open one eye, casually stretch,
Don't jump- but there's no doubt
I'm over the moon to see her
(Try to hide it to no avail)
I look blasé to the point of indifference but-
She can tell by the thump of my tail!

She never gives me enough to eat
She's a really frugal mummy
She says she is worried since I've been spayed
I will grow a big fat tummy!
But I'm far too busy fulfilling my quest,
searching the stream- every stretch,
For discarded balls to enhance our walks
With a game of kick, throw or fetch!
This means I'm perpetually muddy
so she hoses till I'm soggy and sad
when I shake on the doorstep or inside the house
she makes me feel guilty and bad!

But often she gives me a treat or a bone
And then she is happy to play
I pretend to offer her a bite or a chew

Then I growl, snatch and run away!
And when she is feeling lonely or sad
And tearful, or angry and vexed
I climb gently up onto her lap
Put my paws around her neck
And kiss her face, she hugs me tight
And then, I know, I've got it right.

Lament

I dropped her dog
I dropped her dog!!!
It wasn't on purpose, it wasn't meant,
It really was an accident.
(CHORUS)
I dropped her dog
I dropped her dog
I'm sosostorry
I dropped her dog.

She was so small
Not grown at all
So small so sweet
With tiny feet
And tiny paws with tiny claws
And tiny teeth in tiny jaws.
(Chorus)

I dropped her dog
I felt so bad
The worst thing I could do to make her sad
I dropped her dog
I dropped her dog
I'm sosostorry
I dropped her dog.

She was the mate
With whom I'd travel from
east to west the world
unravel
I helped her through
A replacement hip
By walking the kids to school
For a bit
I wanted to be a
Reliable friend, a friend
On which you could depend
But then I went and dropped her dog
I'm sososorry
I dropped her dog.

Whatever my strengths
Whatever my charms
That pup won't
Fly back to my arms.
CHORUS
I've offered to pay
The bill for the vet
She accepted but hasn't
Amounted it yet.
I've done what I can
To make amends
But this could be where the
Friendship ends.
(Chorus)

ER

Dad always said, “She’s the same age as me!”
Both born in 1926
But she had two birthdays where he had only one.
On Christmas day everything stopped
The family were hushed,
And we all listened to her words to the nation.
My parents didn’t live in a palace,
Or die in a castle,
But they had a comfortable house and grew rhubarb and strawberries and runner beans in the garden.
He died when he was ninety one
She was ninety six
Mum was only seventy five.
They would have been sad
To lose someone that had been there all their lives, and ours.
It really is the end of an era.
RIP Elizabeth R.

8th Sept 22

When Lightning Strikes (Golf at Whitby)

"When the dark skies meet the corn,
Always expect a thunderstorm,"
The Lady Captain said,
"If you hear a claxon,
Don't stop to put your macs on,
Just get back here instead."

Our turn to tee off one by one,
Eventually came by,
We set off down the first fairway,
With one eye on the sky.
Hole three when Lynn was on the tee,
The beach and sea below,
White horses riding high and fast
Black clouds began to grow,
And the wind grew cold and now and then
Some drops of rain would tumble
Until we heard the ominous sound
A distant, solitary rumble.
We could have chosen to walk back in
The clubhouse, on hole four,
But felt unwilling to stop, although
The rain began to pour.

(196 footballer, John White,
Was only twenty seven,
Struck by lightning playing golf
And went straight up to heaven.
Mary's father had a cow
Whose fate was just the same.
He could not sell its finest meat
and make insurance claim.)

We trundled trolleys over the bridge,
A trepidacious hike, and
As Mary swung her driver high,
The lightning began to strike.
We ran and hid below the cliff,
Trying to take cover,
thinking we could still play on
When the storm was over.

The rain became torrential and
We all got wetter and wetter,
So diplomatically agreed that
A return for home was better.

Although it's sad to just give up
Go home for early dinners
Lynn and I were both convinced
We would have been the winners.

6th September 2022

Eye rhyme: a homophone, in reverse. Looks the same but sounds different : a crossword clue on that day!

Socks

"You're wearing odd socks!"
My friends all mocked
"You must be growing old!"
It's not the first time I've been told.
But I still hold my head up high
Knowing I have a smart reply
"Stop taking the mickey-if you please
I've a pair at home the same as these!"

Twin's opinion

"Why do they call you Julia?
That sounds really poor,
Why don't they all realise
"Gran" suits you so much more!"

Alexa

When you are only five years old,
(This fact is always true)
The only rude words that you know
Are bottom, fart and poo.
Do we ever grow out of this?
(Just take yourselves to task)
Because Alexa plays the “Poo Poo” song,
Whenever the twins will ask!

The Munchkins

"I'm hungry,
So hungry,"
(Though they've just eaten lunch)
"Haven't you anything, Gran,
on which we can munch?"

(Deep breath, and tongue firmly in cheek)
"I've bananas, apples and oranges too,
Jam with no pips in especially for you!
"I've Peppa Pig Pasta, small grapes with no
seeds,
Toast with yellow butter to meet all your needs!"

"We're not THAT sort of hungry!"
Their hopeful gaze still lingers,
A plea to raid my secret stache- mini cheddars
and chocolate fingers!

Hypomimia

Why didn't I notice her face?
Today, now, I'd have thought she had filler,
Please look closely at the ones you love, when
They're becoming iller and iller.

I've known her face since she was born,
Witnessed every expression,
Smiles, laughter, tears, temper,
Always left an impression.

She studied drama, loved to act
Her whole life was a stage
I missed the clue written on her face
Because of her young age.

The slowness, the limp, the tremors?
What was the cause, we would ask?
Whiplash from a crash? A mild TIA?
But I should have guessed from the mask.

Dr. Specialist knew much more than I,
diagnosing her with ease,
She only needed to walk in the room
To be told, "Parkinson's disease."

That was when she was only forty one
Should have had many years still ahead
To travel, perform, to dance and to sing
But she's trapped in a home instead.

For a few hours a day she's my sister once more
Full of humour, and almost at ease
But for hours and days and years and years
She just fights with this dreadful disease.

(There is still no cure, and my baby sister has been trapped with this disease for over fifteen years. It is progressive. She has no escape.)

Funeral weekend

The wind blows from the east
The nights grow cold and long
The fruit falls prostate on the ground
To tell us she has gone

In London people queue and walk
For thirty hours or more
To tiptoe past the coffin
Of the monarch they adore
She was no pop or film star
No president elect
But everyone's mum, nan, great gran
Commanding our respect
By her loyalty and duty
Even when her end grew nearer
Many will say we all have lived
Through history's finest era.

You may not be a monarchist
Or fly your flag half mast
But take a moment to appreciate
A great queen of the past.

My sister (the other one!)

We drink the wine
We chew the fat
We put the world to rights
The nearer we get to the grave
The more we seem to misbehave
We laugh and joke and dance and sing
Take all the world under our wing
Assist each other's flights.

We pour more wine
We make a feast
We put together plans
Of places we would like to see
In far and distant lands.

We take our dogs
We climb the hills
Or stroll along a beach
And reminisce
Of times long past
That now seem out of reach.

Some glad, some sad,
some mad, some bad,
Reminders shared and spoken,

And she and I, live to defy-
We try to fly and still aim high
And no doubt will until we die-
While others have been broken.

We always know between us
We have someone to rely on,
With whom to share a well-worn joke
A shoulder we can cry on

I worry about who'll go first,
It should be me, I know,
So sad to leave her on her own
But I'd hate to be left alone
Because I'm sure I'd miss her
My mad, loud, crazy sister.
(Love you lots)

Ode to Alcohol 2

When I was feeling so alone,
You cheered me up, you warmed my home,
And when I could not sleep in fear,
You hummed a lullaby in my ear.
You smoothed anxiety from my brow,
Enabled my confidence to grow,
You made me feel alive, slim, pretty,
And all my jokes seemed twice as witty.

You kept me always wanting more,
I was your prostitute, your whore,
Not caring much from whence you came-
As long as your love stayed the same.
Perhaps because I was so needy,
I wanted more; became too greedy,
My waist grew thick, my skin grew dry,
A furtive look within my eye.
I made excuses, stayed indoors,
My craven company; only yours.

Now you had me in your grip,
Your loving smile began to slip.
Once I had become your wife,
You then went on to wreck my life.

You stole my money, clipped my wings,
Forced me to say such terrible things,
Made me clumsy, made me dread,
Distorted reason in my head.
You broke my sleep, for hours I'd pace,
Until the day I'd have to face,
With red, bruised eyes and burning pain,
Like flushing acid down a drain;
Each day I'd vow to turf you out,
But come the evening, I would doubt
That I could manage on my own-
Even you were better than being alone.

So things continued worse and worse,
I slumbered under Aurora's curse,
Woke heavy- hearted every morning,
Then it came- a final warning.

A shock that made me realise,
And dragged the blindfold from my eyes,
Revealed the truth behind your lies-
You were an enemy in disguise.

When old love sours, let new begin-
I chucked the bottles in the bin.

Tennis rap

Swing low to high
Swing low to high
Topspin balls will touch the sky

Follow through
Follow through
The ball will go where you want it to!

Raise racquet head
Raise racquet head
Ready to kill those serves stone dead

Squeeze and freeze
Squeeze and freeze
Put those volleys away with ease!

Racquet tap
Racquet tap
Encourage your partner like a clap

Feet should jiggle
Feet should jiggle
Distract your opponent, make them giggle

Point and stare
Point and stare
Smash that ball right through the air

Shake and smile
Shake and smile
Because
Good sports always end with style!

www.ingramcontent.com/pod-product-compliance
Lightning Source LLC
Chambersburg PA
CBHW051747130826
49812CB00033B/1037
* 9 7 8 9 3 9 5 9 5 0 7 2 5 *